LITTLE BOOK OF
BEES

THE LITTLE BOOK OF BEES

An Hachette UK Company
www.hachette.co.uk

Summersdale Publishers Ltd
Part of Octopus Publishing Group Limited
Carmelite House
50 Victoria Embankment
LONDON
EC4Y 0DZ
UK

www.summersdale.com

Printed and bound in China

ISBN: 978-1-78783-988-5

Substantial discounts on bulk quantities of Summersdale books are available to corporations, professional associations and other organizations. For details contact general enquiries: telephone: +44 (0) 1243 771107 or email: enquiries@summersdale.com.

The

LITTLE BOOK OF

BEES

Vicki Vrint

With thanks to all at Tuppenny Barn Organics and Education for their ongoing work to ensure the protection of bees. Particular thanks to Adrian Pert, beekeeping instructor, for honeybee wisdom.

CONTENTS

THE HUM OF BEES IS THE VOICE OF THE GARDEN.

ELIZABETH LAWRENCE

Introduction

Bees have been around for over 100 million years, and in that time they've found a home in almost every part of the globe. There are over 20,000 species of bee, but most well-known bee facts relate specifically to honeybees, owing to our close relationship with this hive-dwelling species. In fact, around half of the planet's bee species are solitary, most don't make or store honey, and they can look very different to the yellow-and-black bees we're familiar with.

The Little Book of Bees explores and celebrates all things "bee" – their surprising abilities; their place in folklore and culture; their essential role as pollinators; and the things we can do to look after them.

It's a sad fact that these wonderfully adaptive insects, who've survived a whole host of changes since they first appeared on our planet, are now under serious threat. With around one-third of bee species in decline, it's a critical time for us to do everything we can to support them. This book will leave you buzzing with enthusiasm for these brilliant and beautiful creatures and, more importantly, with ideas for how to help them.

BEE BASICS

Most of our encounters with bees in the wild are a brief buzzing fly-by as they dip into flower after flower – wonderful moments, but they don't give us the time to observe the fascinating details of our favourite pollinators' lives. This chapter helps us to get better acquainted with the different species of bee, their life cycle and their amazing anatomy.

Different types of bee

Bees belong to the Hymenoptera order of insects, which also includes ants and wasps – in fact, it's believed that bees descended from wasps around 130 million years ago, as we'll see in Chapter 2. Bees have been around for so long that they've had time to evolve into the planet's top pollinators and to diversify into thousands of different species, each adapted to find pollen in its own environmental niche.

Honeybees (of which there are seven species) and bumblebees (250 species worldwide) are eusocial. This means that they live in colonies and work together as a unit, dividing up tasks between them. Honeybee colonies hunker down together for the winter, using their stores of honey to get by, but bumblebee colonies survive for just one season, with the new queens alone hibernating underground ready to start their next colony in the spring.

Most bee species don't live in such a highly organized and cooperative way, though. Communal bee species raise their own young separately inside a nest with a shared entrance, while other species live in aggregations (having separate nests in the same area), but the vast majority of bees are truly solitary. They nest alone (often underground) in locations as diverse as railway embankments, cliff faces, gardens, allotments and even seashells.

At the opposite end of the scale to the hard-working team-player honeybees are the "cuckoo" bees. As their name suggests, these bees, which belong to several different species, infiltrate other species' nests and lay their eggs in them. On hatching, their larvae will do away with the nests' true occupants and feed on the pollen supplies stashed there. This is why adult cuckoo bees don't have pollen-collecting hairs – they let other parents do all the hard work of pollen gathering.

The bee life cycle

Bees begin life as an egg, hatch as a small white larva and then eat nectar and pollen voraciously until they're big enough to spin a cocoon. The larval stage lasts around two weeks in bumblebees, but can take longer for other species. Once inside their cocoon, the grub-like larvae transform into adult bees and emerge ready to face the world.

Most bees live for a single season, starting their adult life in spring with one mission in mind – reproduction. For male bees this means mating, so they must track down females and vie with one another for the chance to mate. (If successful, male honeybees and bumblebees die after mating.)

Meanwhile, female solitary bees build their nest and store enough pollen and nectar for their offspring to feed on when they hatch. They mate, lay around 20 eggs then seal them away. The larvae feast on pollen then hide in their cocoon for up to 11 months, emerging in the spring.

For females in colonies, life is a little different. Reproductive duties and larvae care will be shared between the queen and her workers respectively.

BUMBLEBEE LIFE CYCLE

At the end of the summer, new queens are raised by the bumblebee colony. They must mate and then lie dormant for the winter, ready to start their own colonies in the spring. If they make it through the winter, the queens must find suitable places to build their nests – perhaps a nook under a shed, a hollow tree or an abandoned rodent nest. Each queen lays her eggs in a sticky pollen ball and sits on them until they hatch into the colony's first worker bees. (All workers are female, but the queen is the only bee who can lay eggs.) The queen continues to lay eggs, which hatch into workers raised by their sisters. Later in the season the queen produces male bees and new queens ready to continue the cycle, before she dies. Apart from the new queens, the colony dies off at the end of the season.

HONEYBEE LIFE CYCLE

When new queens emerge from their cells they head out to mate. They make just one "mating flight", pairing with around ten to 15 drones, and will store enough sperm from this for a lifetime of egg-laying. The more drones a queen mates with, the greater the genetic variation and strength of the hive. The queen lays eggs in hexagonal cells of honeycomb built by the workers, who raise the larvae and maintain the hive. The workers feed the larvae rich royal jelly at first, followed by pollen and honey until they are ready to pupate, then the workers seal them into their cells ready to transform into adult bees. The queen can either lay fertilized eggs (which will turn into female workers) or unfertilized ones, which will become male drones. A productive queen can lay 1,000–1,500 eggs a day during honey season and can live up to five years.

BEE PRODUCTS

HONEY – The sweet substance made from nectar and stored by honeybees (and a few other species) to sustain the colony throughout the winter.

NECTAR – The sugary liquid found in many flowering plants. It attracts bees to the flower for pollination, and provides them with a valuable energy source.

POLLEN – While nectar provides energy, pollen provides protein for growing bees. Adults turn pollen into pollen cakes to feed baby bees.

PROPOLIS – This sticky substance is made from sap and used by honeybees as a sealant in their hive.

ROYAL JELLY – A super-nutritious food made by honeybees for newly hatched larvae. Extra quantities are used to create new queen bees.

WAX – Secreted by female honeybees, wax is used to build their hive and seal in nectar cells. Bumblebee queens also make wax and use it to construct small nectar pots and cover their eggs.

Bee anatomy

Bees are highly evolved and adapted for a life flitting from flower to flower. Here's a look at their anatomy: what makes a bee, a bee?

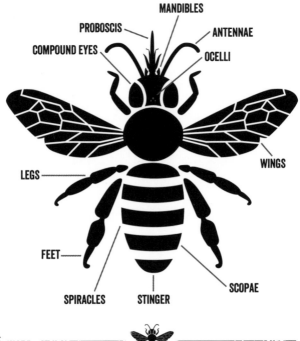

MANDIBLES

PROBOSCIS

ANTENNAE

COMPOUND EYES

OCELLI

WINGS

LEGS

FEET

SCOPAE

SPIRACLES

STINGER

The ocelli – the three eyes on top of a bee's head – are for navigation. They register light, but not shapes. They're also used for detecting when a predator is approaching from above.

Bees also have two large compound eyes, made up of thousands of tiny lenses, which show them their surroundings as little dots of colour. They cannot see red, but they can detect ultraviolet light instead, which helps them target flowers. These compound eyes are hairy – it's believed the hairs detect wind direction.

A bee's mandibles (jaw) are used for everything from carrying pollen and feeding larvae to fighting and gripping.

Most of a bee's information about their surroundings comes from their antennae. These have thousands of tiny sensors that are extremely sensitive and primed to pick up the scent of different flowers. The antennae are also used to touch and taste, as well as to detect weather conditions.

Bees may have long or short tongues, depending on the type of flowers their species tends to visit. Long-tongued bees suck up nectar through their tubular proboscis, while short-tongued bees lap it up.

Bees have two pairs of interlocking wings, which beat in a figure-of-eight pattern at around 230 beats per second in flight, creating that familiar buzzing sound. They're so efficient at carrying loads that scientists are hoping to model a hovering aircraft on their flight methods.

Bees' legs are adapted for different tasks, and are segmented and flexible. The front and middle pairs are used to clean their antennae of pollen – the front pair even have a special notch just for this purpose. The back pair of legs can be used for cleaning wings, and – in honeybees and bumblebees – also has handy pouches, called corbiculae, which the foraging bees fill with pollen.

Bees have tarsal claws on their feet to help them grip, and display a preference for petals with conical cells that act like Velcro, making it easier to feed. They have taste receptors on the ends of their legs, and – thanks to the scent that their feet leave behind – can work out whether friends, relatives or other bees have landed on the flower or leaf before them.

Only female bees have a sting in the tail, as their stinger has evolved from their egg-laying tube. Honeybees generally die after they sting – their barbed stinger is pulled away when the bee tries to retract it through tough mammalian skin – but most other bee species have a barbless stinger that can be used time and again. Honeybee queens, however, have a smaller stinger, which they can use repeatedly – usually against other queens.

Like many other insects, bees have openings in their side called spiracles, and they breathe through these, drawing air straight through their exoskeleton to where it's needed.

Bees are covered in pollen-collecting hairs called scopae. The hairs differ, depending on the type of pollen the bee collects: wider hairs are efficient for capturing larger grains of pollen. Older honeybees can become rather bald, after working hard collecting pollen and crawling through the passageways in their hive, rubbing up against other bees.

Amazing abilities

Our long-standing fascination with bees has led to some amazing discoveries about their abilities.

It was Nobel prizewinner Karl von Frisch who decoded the honeybees' waggle dance, an intricate series of moves they use to communicate information about good sources of nectar or water to their hive-mates. The dance involves a combination of waggles, which show distance, and turns, which indicate direction, to the location in question. More recently, researchers have discovered that different species of honeybee use a different "dialect" of dance, but bees are so smart that Asiatic bees could translate the dance of their European cousins.

Honeybees are brilliant communicators in other ways, too. They use sound signals to encourage other bees to get to work, by vibrating their abdomens and either gripping on to their lazy comrade or flying around the hive to pass on the message. This drumming sound has been shown to increase hive activity. Other signals bees make include a whooping noise to express surprise and a sound to request grooming from their sisters. Honeybees also secrete oily pheromones, leaving a trail that alerts other bees to food sources.

But honeybees aren't the only smart cookies of the apian world. Solitary bees can check out other bees' nests for signs of parasitic infection and then avoid them when picking their own nesting place. When researchers used symbols to mark infected nests, they noticed that bees were able to recognize them and avoid them in the future – what amazing cognitive ability!

Bees are a rare example of invertebrates who can use tools. They were able to push a ball into a hole in return for a nectar reward, learning quickly when they saw a fake bee – a plastic model created by scientists – do the task. They were able to think creatively when the puzzle was changed, too. All this from creatures with a brain no bigger than a mustard seed!

BEES DANCE IN THE
DARK TO GIVE OTHER BEES
ACCURATE INFORMATION...
A FEAT OF COMMUNICATION
RIVALLED ONLY BY HUMAN
LANGUAGE ITSELF.

RICHARD DAWKINS

Baffling bee facts

- 34°C (93°F) – the temperature inside a beehive
- 200–400 – the number of bumblebees in a colony
- 10,000–60,000 – the number of honeybees in a hive
- 6 million – the number of sperm a honeybee queen will store in her body for life
- 1 million – the number of brain cells a bee has (a human has 1 billion)
- 25 km/h (16 mph) – the speed at which a honeybee can fly
- 1/12 of a teaspoon – the amount of honey one bee will make in its lifetime

AVERAGE LIFE EXPECTANCY:

- 2–6 weeks – worker bumblebee
- 6 weeks – honeybee worker (summer)
- 8 weeks – honeybee drone
- 5 months – honeybee worker (winter)
- 4–6 months – solitary bee
- 1 year – bumblebee queen
- 3–4 years – honeybee queen

Bee species

There are seven families of bee, which include a huge variety of species. They range from the world's smallest, *Perdita minima*, at 2 mm (0.07 in.) long, which nests in sandy desert areas in the southwest of the US, to the largest, *Megachile pluto* (40 mm/1½ in. long), a bee so rare that it was believed to be extinct until its recent rediscovery in Indonesia. The seven bee families are:

One of the biggest families, the *Andrenidae* are mining bees: solitary bees who dig nests in the earth, and lay their eggs in individual cells. An easy-to-spot example found across Europe is the tawny mining bee. Bright orange females leave a volcano-like mound in the lawn when they've been digging.

Mostly found in South America and Australia, the *Colletidae* are known as plasterer bees since they waterproof their nests with a cellophane-like secretion. An unusual example found in southern Australia is the bright orange-and-black-striped wasp mimic bee, who seals the entrance to her nest with a curtain of "cellophane" strands.

The *Halictidae*, or sweat bees, are a family of bees common in the US, but found around the world. Easy to spot with their flashes of metallic green, blue or yellow, they're attracted to the salt in human sweat. A new species, *Lasioglossum gothami*, was recently identified in New York City.

The *Megachilidae* family are ingenious builders who use materials around them to construct nests inside existing cavities. They include mason bees (who use mud), carder bees (who use plant and animal fibre), leafcutter bees and resin bees. In the UK, the patchwork leafcutter can be found trimming neat patches of rose or wisteria leaves, which she'll form into cells for her eggs.

The *Melittidae* is a small but ancient family of bees most commonly found in Africa. Many have evolved to collect flower oils as well as pollen, which they mix to feed their larvae, or use to line their nests. Some oil-collecting bees are known for their extra-long forelegs, which they use to sponge up plant oils.

Another small bee family is the *Strenotritidae*, found only in Australia. These mining bees are known for being speedy flyers and for having a particularly dense covering of hair. They nest in the ground – with some species digging as deep as 3 m (10 ft) – and they're unusual in that the larvae don't spin cocoons.

Finally, the *Apidae* is the family we're most familiar with as it includes bumblebees and honeybees as well as stingless and carpenter bees.

BUMBLEBEES

Of the 250 bumblebee species worldwide, 24 can be found in Britain, with a "big seven" of these being the most common and recognizable, and there are around 46 species in the US. (Sadly two species have been lost in the UK during the past century and three have gone extinct globally.) Most bumblebees are eusocial, but a few species are "cuckoo bees" (see page 11). Bumblebees get their Latin name from their characteristically loud buzz – *Bombus* means "booming". Tail colour, ranging from white to red, is important when identifying these charming bees. Bumblebees are the gentle giants of the garden and rarely sting – in fact, if provoked, they'll usually raise a leg in warning rather than attack.

> The seven bumblebee species most common in the UK are buff-tailed, white-tailed, early, garden, red-tailed, forest cuckoo and tree bumblebees.

HONEYBEES

There are seven main species of honeybee – the most common being *Apis mellifera* (the European honeybee). Honeybees are fascinating because of the high level of cooperation that takes place in each colony, which can number 50,000 inhabitants or more. All a bee's efforts are devoted to the survival of the colony, with every bee doing its duty, even if that means giving its life for the good of the hive. The queen spends her time laying eggs – she is shepherded from one cell to another by a group of attendants who keep an eye on her progress. If she is judged to be ineffective, workers can prepare new queen cells and arrange for her to be deposed!

The hive is mostly populated by worker bees – infertile females – who take on a range of tasks throughout their lives, including basic cleaning, feeding larvae, cell building and repair, storing pollen and making honey, maintaining the hive temperature, guard duties and foraging. During the height of summer, these bees work so hard that their life expectancy is just five or six weeks.

The final type of bee found in the hive is the drone – during breeding season there are several hundred of these in the hive. The drones are male and their sole role is to mate, so they make regular flights to Drone Congregation Areas (DCAs) on the hunt for visiting queens. In comparison with the busy workers, they may not seem to contribute much toward hive maintenance, but they do help to cool the hive temperature by flapping their wings if things get too heated, and they bring essential genetic diversity to bee colonies. (A queen may mate with up to 20 drones on her mating flight, and will store this sperm in her body to use throughout her lifetime.) Drones are expelled from the hive before winter as they would be an unnecessary drain on valuable resources.

A HISTORY
OF BEES

The history of bees takes us from their beginnings in humid prehistoric climes to their place as the top pollinators on the planet today. Closely entwined with the evolution of flowers – as well as the development of humans – it's a tale that includes sneaky blooms, brilliant beekeepers... and the accidental creation of a killer hybrid along the way.

The evolution of bees

The story of bees begins in the Cretaceous period, amid dinosaurs and ancient forests. The early ancestors of birds and butterflies shared airspace with prehistoric flying insects, including wasps – and bees are descended from one of these wasp species. Wasps are carnivorous, and stocked their nests with insect prey for their offspring to feed on. Many of those unfortunate insects would have fed on pollen, and been covered in it too. Bees evolved when some wasps developed a taste for pollen alone, and left their carnivorous ways behind.

Bee fossils are rare, but a few of their early ancestors have been discovered trapped in amber. One found recently in Myanmar shows a transitional form from wasp to bee, while the oldest known bee fossil is of a stingless bee from 80 million years ago. DNA sequencing suggests that bees first appeared 130 million years ago – it's no coincidence that this was when the first flowering plants developed.

THE BEE'S LIFE IS LIKE A MAGIC WELL: THE MORE YOU DRAW FROM IT, THE MORE IT FILLS WITH WATER.

KARL VON FRISCH

A close relationship

The development of bees is closely linked with the evolution of flowers, as bees are solely dependent on pollen and nectar for their survival. When the bees' carnivorous ancestors were taking to the skies, most plants were still reliant on wind pollination. (For a plant to reproduce, the pollen – male seeds – from one plant must be transferred to the female reproductive parts of another.) The chances of pollen finding its target using this hit-or-miss method were pretty slim, so plants produced vast quantities of the stuff... and flying insects began to feed on it. As they visited plant after plant, they transferred the pollen on their bodies, and a much more efficient system of pollination developed.

Early plants were not the bright, many-petalled flowers we're familiar with today, but it soon became an advantage for plants to do all they could to attract pollinators. Dull green and brown plants developed coloured petals, competing with one another to produce large numbers of brighter blooms, and some offered nectar, too – an extra sweet incentive to entice pollinators to visit. The nectar was cunningly tucked away so that insects would have to delve deep or squeeze down narrow passageways in order to get to it – providing better pollination. In turn, these visitors, particularly bees, developed longer tongues to suck up their reward. And so bee and flower species evolved in tandem, with different bees specializing in pollinating different species and shapes of plant.

Cheating the system

Both bees and flowers have evolved to try to get their rewards in the most efficient way possible. Snapdragons are rather sneaky: they hide their pollen under a petal and it only pops out when a bee lands on the flower and its weight triggers its release. Many flowers use bright ultraviolet patterns to act as targets leading the bees to their prize.

Bees and flowers don't always play fair when it comes to pollination: some bees bite through the sides of tubular flowers and take a shortcut to their nectar prize. Meanwhile, some plants give every sign of having nectar, but don't actually provide any once the bee has landed, ensuring pollination without expending any energy in return.

Some flowers go to even greater lengths to attract bees, making an addictive caffeine-type nectar, sweetening their nectar when they detect vibrations from passing bees or even – in the case of the bee orchid – mimicking the appearance and smell of another bee in order to attract a passing male to "mate" with it.

Honey hunting

It's no wonder that our prehistoric ancestors went to great lengths to get hold of honey: it's a valuable source of energy and finding it could make all the difference to survival in a hunter-gatherer society. Early humans would cut down trees – or climb them – to plunder bees' nests and steal honeycomb. Cave paintings from the Mesolithic era depict honey hunters at work, climbing trees in search of precious comb.

Honey hunters used cunning methods to track down bees' nests: looking out for their droppings on leaves; or capturing bees, coating them in flour or ochre, and then tracking them. In Aboriginal culture, honey hunting was a female role, with trackers tying a feather to a bee in order to follow it to its nest. In some areas, honey hunting is still a tradition today and a source of income for those skilled at finding nests, but most honey is obtained from kept bees – something humans have been doing for thousands of years.

Early beekeeping

As our hunter-gatherer ancestors started to settle in fertile areas and nurture crops of fruit, vegetables and grains, wild bee populations flourished. It's a sad irony that our first steps in agriculture benefitted bees, whereas today's intensive methods are having a negative impact on their numbers (see page 78). As bees were drawn to the crops surrounding settlements, the inhabitants realized the value of keeping them close at hand and provided early hives to house the bees, so that they could harvest honey.

Archaeologists have found evidence of beeswax being used 8,000 years ago and of beekeeping at least 3,000 years ago in the Middle East: stone carvings from Egypt show that a honey industry was flourishing on the banks of the Nile. But we have even more evidence of the Egyptians' beekeeping spoils – jars of the honey itself! Because of its low water content, honey doesn't spoil, and perfectly preserved jars have been found sealed away in tombs from several thousand years ago. We also know that the ancient Egyptians used smoke to pacify bees when they were working on the hives.

The Egyptians were not alone in keeping – and revering – bees. The ancient Mayans used hives built from hollowed-out logs with stone discs as stoppers, while the Romans made detailed notes on the most profitable way to keep bees and harvest honey. In China, the business benefits of beekeeping were recorded during the East-Han dynasty (25–150 CE) and there are references to the sacred role of honey and mead in the Hindu *Rig-Veda* too.

"Nectar of the gods"

Seen in early societies as sacred, honey played an important part in many ceremonies and rituals, and was even used to preserve the dead. It was also used as a commodity – for payment of taxes – and as a medicine, since it has antibacterial qualities and is effective for treating wounds. Until refined sugar became an affordable alternative for most people, in the 1700s, honey was also the only sweetener available.

Early Christians believed bees were a model of industry: hard-working, productive and – they thought – virginal. Because of this, they saw all bee products as pure and eminently suitable for use. This is one reason why most monasteries and convents had apiaries. There was also a huge demand for beeswax in candle-making – not only was it considered godly, but it created a sweet-smelling alternative to the pungent tallow candles used by ordinary folk. With all these treasures on offer, it's easy to see why beekeeping was an important activity in most communities.

Beekeeping through the ages

Tree-beekeeping was one early way of earning a supply of valuable honey: medieval beekeepers would nurture and harvest nests that they found in trees, or create optimum conditions for bees to take up home in them, even going so far as to create whole bee forests. But it was soon discovered that it was less time-consuming and complicated to keep bees in hives, closer to home, and so hive beekeeping became the popular method that is still used today.

The only difference from one area to another was the type of hive used. Log hives were a natural progression from tree-beekeeping, and are still used in parts of Africa today. In other areas, beehives were constructed from whatever materials were easily available – in Egypt they were woven with twigs and reeds and covered with sun-dried clay. In Greece, hives were often built from terracotta and in Portugal, where cork trees are abundant, the hives are made from a cylinder of cork bark. In the UK and US skeps were – and still are – a traditional hive option; they are woven from coils of straw or reeds.

The downside of many of these early hive designs was that there was no way for the beekeeper to access or check on their bees – and harvesting the honey from skeps often involved poisoning the bees with sulphur first. By the nineteenth century, though, beekeepers would drive the bees from one skep to another by drumming on the side of their existing home and placing an empty basket above it to encourage the bees to move house, leaving the honey harvest behind.

Human friends and foes

Humans haven't always used bees for benign purposes. They've also been employed as a form of defence: Virgil stored his valuables in his beehive to deter looters and it's claimed that nuns at the convent in Beyenburg ("Beetown") in Germany set loose their bees to see off a band of intruders.

Sadly bees have been used as weapons in the past, with hives of enraged bees being hurled into enemy territory on land and at sea. Poisoned honey and drugged mead have played a part in human hostilities too. In modern times, scientists have taken advantage of bees' highly developed sense of smell, training them to detect drugs and explosives. Meanwhile, our beekeeping practices have affected bee populations: when Europeans migrated to the Americas and Australasia, the European honeybee went with them, and so *Apis mellifera* spread its wings even farther afield.

Humans have sought to selectively breed bees – not an easy task when mating takes place on the wing – but one success story took place at Buckfast Abbey in 1916, after the hives were hit by "Isle of Wight disease". Brother Adam, the beekeeper, bred a bee that was resistant to the chronic infection by travelling the world to find suitable honeybees to use. His "Buckfast Superbee" remains the bee of choice for commercial honey producers today. With infection being a key factor in the recent decline in bee numbers, breeding disease-resistant bees is something that entomologists are considering again.

In 1956, Warwick Kerr hoped to create more productive honeybees by importing African honeybees to his Brazil lab. When some escaped and bred with European honeybees, Kerr's accidental hybrid was unleashed – an aggressive strain of Africanized honeybee, whose enthusiastic defence of their hive has gained them the nickname "killer bees". Despite their portrayal in B movies, Africanized bees don't deserve quite such a harsh reputation. They aren't out to destroy the human race, but will defend their nest aggressively and in large numbers if provoked.

Bee science

Bees have fascinated humans for as long as they've lived alongside them. Aristotle studied bees in an observation hive as long ago as 350 BCE. Some of his deductions were a little off-beam, though: he thought that the queen bee was a king, and that bees found their young in flowers, rather than laying eggs!

Pioneering naturalist Reverend Gilbert White described his experiment to see if bees can hear in his 1789 book *The Natural History of Selborne*. He bellowed at his beehives through a speaking trumpet. The bees were completely undisturbed by this incident, and carried on their business as normal.

In the US, beekeeper Reverend L. L. Langstroth realized that bees fill smaller spaces in their hive with propolis, but larger gaps are bridged with valuable honeycomb. Using this knowledge, he perfected the Langstroth hive, and 75 per cent of all hives used today are still based on his design.

Charles Darwin was fascinated by bees, and enlisted his children to help him track their flight paths through his garden. He also spent a lot of time observing the building of honeycomb, concluding that the efficient method they use to construct their comb was the product of millions of years of evolution.

Bees' selfless behaviour and dedication to the colony as a whole has been studied at length. Scientists believe this cooperation is due to worker bees sharing more DNA with their sisters than they would with potential offspring – a theory that provided part of the inspiration for Richard Dawkins' "selfish gene" view of evolution.

Bee biology and behaviour has continued to fascinate entomologists. In 2018, Tim Landgraf built a waggle-dancing robot to study bee communication in greater depth, and concerned entomologists the world over are turning their attention to the challenges that bees are facing, building high-tech smart hives to monitor bees more closely and hopefully slow their decline.

Beekeeping today

Beekeeping has become a popular pastime, offering people a chance to reconnect with nature and a traditional way of life. Widespread reports of bee decline have also raised awareness of the bees' plight and led to a rise in urban beekeeping, with hives finding homes on roof terraces and in backyards. Bees are big business. In addition to honey and beeswax, we use propolis, royal jelly and pollen in beauty products, medicines and foods (see page 70), but the most valuable gift bees give us continues to be pollination. With almost 80 per cent of our main crops dependent on insect pollination, many farmers use commercial hives. Migratory beekeepers tour the US every year with lorries laden with pallets of hives – a controversial practice due to the impact on the local wild bee population and the risk of spreading disease.

Today more than ever bees need our support, but if we work together to combine traditional wisdom, good commercial practice and a dash of scientific knowledge – along with our affection for these special insects – we can improve their outlook.

BEES IN FOLKLORE, LEGEND AND CULTURE

Humans have had a relationship with bees (and honey) for thousands of years, so it's no surprise that bees have always held great spiritual and cultural significance for us. In this chapter we discover bee lore and legend and find these amazing insects appearing in everything from ancient myths to modern movies.

Spiritual beliefs

Bees have a place in the myths and sacred places of most ancient cultures, from Africa to Australia and India to South America. The ancient Egyptians believed bees were a divine gift from Re, the sun god – born of his tears. Bees were associated with royalty, and the bee was the symbol of the king of Lower Egypt. Jars of honey were sealed into tombs for deceased pharaohs to use in the afterlife, and Roman, Hindu and Chinese cultures all had burial rituals concerning honeybees. In Indian, ancient Near East and Aegean cultures, the bee was believed to bridge the living world with the underworld, the mythical abode of the dead.

Bees play a part in the creation story of the Kombumerri people of the Gold Coast, in which Dreaming God Jabreen became hungry after sculpting the land to create rivers and mountains. He feasted on sticky honey from wild bees, but had to swim in the ocean to wash himself clean, then fell asleep. His body created the mountain Jellurgal, "place of honey and place of bees".

A creation story of the Kalahari Bushmen tells that humanity was born of Bee, who had selflessly carried Mantis on her back across a raging river. Buffeted by winds, Bee sank exhausted onto a beautiful flower floating on the torrent, delivering Mantis to safety. Bee died, but when the sun rose, the first human was discovered in her place, curled up in the flower.

A chapter of the Quran – 1,400 years ago – was ahead of its time in referring to bees in the feminine. Bees are mentioned in the Bible too, with a swarm appearing in the carcass of Samson's slaughtered lion to symbolize the victory of good over evil. There are also many biblical references to honey as a symbol of purity. Meanwhile, the word for "bee" and "pure" in Turkish is the same – *arı*.

Seen as a gift of the gods, honey crops up in many myths. In one Greek legend, the nymph Melissa nurtured the baby Zeus with milk and honey, while a Brazilian myth describes why honeycomb can be found high up in trees. It explains that honey was originally found in pots on the ground but the gods became angry at how lazy humans were, feasting on it so easily. They commanded the bees to build their honeycomb high up, so that we would have to work hard for our reward!

Mead, which is fermented from honey, water and yeast, has been used for ceremonial and celebratory purposes for thousands of years. In fact, it was being brewed 6,000 years ago, making it one of our most ancient alcoholic drinks. As nectar of the gods, it was believed to imbue the drinker with special powers - including wisdom, immortality, fertility and the gift of poetry - and there are dozens of myths surrounding this potent beverage.

Bees - and mead - were believed to bring wisdom as bees were thought to be the messengers of the gods. There's a tradition in the western isles of Scotland that the bees still possess the knowledge of the Druids, so we should "Ask the wild bee for what the Druid knew." In Norse mythology, the Mead of Poetry was said to turn anyone who drank it into a scholar or a poet, and thanks to this tale, any words uttered by mead-befuddled Anglo-Saxons at a gathering in the mead hall were believed to be wise and true! In other legends, however, mead was used to dull the senses of unfortunate victims of the gods.

Superstitions

Bees feature in swarms of superstitions from across the world. The best known here in the West is the practice of "telling the bees" the news of any birth, marriage or death that happens within the family. If a household didn't keep their bees informed by whispering the news to the hives, it was believed that the bees would leave – some folk even went as far as dressing their hives with red cloth for a celebration or black for mourning.

Bees were considered to be sensitive souls who were easily offended by being left out of proceedings, by being exchanged for money – many beehives were gained by bartering – or by overhearing bad language. It was also believed that bees could detect unfaithfulness in men and wantonness in women, and would mark out offenders by stinging them! There was a tradition in central Europe where brides would lead their grooms by a beehive to test their fidelity.

Bees have been used to predict the weather – it was believed that if they stayed close to their hives it was a sign of an approaching storm – and swarms of bees in ancient Rome were thought to precede momentous events. Opinion was divided about whether they were a good or bad sign, but in most superstitions, the arrival of a swarm of bees was considered an omen of death or ill fortune. In some rural areas, the position of a bee swarm in a tree was thought to foretell the price of grain – the higher, the better!

Encounters with individual bees were often signs of good luck. If a bee landed on your head, it meant success would be yours, or if it landed on your hand you would receive money soon. Xhosa tradition, however, teaches that an encounter with a bee brings a message from the ancestors – if the bee stings it's a sure sign that there's something your forebears need you to attend to.

Buzzwords

Bees have been part of our lives for so long that they've acquired some charming folk names along the way, many of these celebrating their special attributes. In Scotland, the moss bee was named the foggy toddler, thanks to its slow bumbling flight. Meanwhile, the buzzing of a bumblebee is captured in names such as hummabee, drumbee, humble-dad and dumbledore – a name borrowed by J. K. Rowling because she imagined that her Hogwarts headmaster could often be found humming to himself.

We've also taken bee names for ourselves: Melissa comes from the Greek word for bee, Deborah is derived from the Hebrew for bee, and Madhukar means bee in Sanskrit.

Of course, there's also plenty of bee terminology to enjoy. Beekeeping is known as apiculture (from the Latin *apis*, for bee), and a beekeeper is an apiarist. There are many words for a group of bees, including a swarm, drift or cast (a smaller swarm), but the traditional collective noun is a "bike" – which meant "swarm" in old English.

Bees have crept into our language in another way – via a host of everyday expressions. We've been referring to busy people as "busy bees" for centuries, and this has led to the word "bee" being used to describe a group of people working together for a single cause – from the corn "husking bees" of colonial times to the spelling and sewing bees of more recent years.

During the 1920s bee-related sayings were very much in vogue – "the bee's knees" meant something impressive; and Cole Porter's song "Let's Do It" popularized the phrase "the birds and the bees", a handy euphemism for something entirely natural but not always mentionable! A bee's ability to return straight to her hive lends us the expression "to make a beeline for" something, while "a bee in your bonnet" refers to the way we can get hung up on an idea that's buzzing around in our head.

Culture

Bees have long been symbols of industry and cooperation – qualities for us humans to aspire to – and so the bee has been adopted as an emblem for various groups. Mormons have been using the symbol of the beehive, which represents unity, since the 1850s. It appears more generally in the US in works of art and on currency and has come to symbolize industriousness and economic success. Meanwhile, the Manchester worker bee has been a symbol of the city since Victorian times; it represents a community whose success has been brought about by the hard work and unity of its residents.

The unusual lifestyle of honeybees has sparked the imagination of writers and film-makers, too. While many of the writers of antiquity made detailed observations and notes on nurturing their bee friends, Virgil went further and waxed lyrical about beekeeping in his epic poem, the *Georgics* (*c*.30 BC). Bees have symbolized unsettling thoughts (Sylvia Plath), or virtue and grace (Carol Ann Duffy). They've inspired acclaimed novels, such as Sue

Monk Kidd's *The Secret Life of Bees*, which spent two and a half years on the *New York Times* bestseller list, plus many other titles, often with a dystopian theme.

Almost every genre of film has been invaded by bees, from animations (*Bee Movie*) and thrillers (*The Swarm*), to drama (*Ulee's Gold*) and dozens of documentaries on the current crisis facing these precious insects (*The Pollinators*). And if reading a novel or watching a movie about bees isn't enough, you can always celebrate them by listening to music. Rimsky-Korsakov's "Flight of the Bumblebee" is wonderfully evocative – and notoriously tricky to play – as it so faithfully captures the speedy sounds of a bumblebee's buzzing flight.

Famous beekeepers

Henry Fonda: A lifelong beekeeper, the renowned actor received a badge for beekeeping as a boy scout and went on to share his Bel Air honey with friends and family.

Scarlett Johansson: Famously received a beehive as a wedding gift, but when nuclear physicist **Dr Eva Crane** received one for her nuptials in 1942, it changed her life: she gave up physics and became a beekeeper and researcher.

Sir Edmund Hillary: A commercial beekeeper by trade, the New Zealand mountaineer's 1,400 hives helped finance his celebrated Everest climb alongside Tenzing Norgay.

Sylvia Plath: Took up beekeeping with enthusiasm and wrote a series of powerful poems in which bees symbolize her mind, abuzz with dark thoughts.

Sherlock Holmes: The fictional detective retired to the South Downs to live among his bees, writing a practical handbook on beekeeping at the same time.

Martha Stewart: The lifestyle guru used honey from her hives in a host of home-cooked recipes.

Leo Tolstoy: The Russian author would spend hours sitting in front of his hives.

Gregor Mendel: The father of genetics turned his attention to bees after peas... but was baffled by the weird and wonderful world of bee reproduction.

Maria von Trapp: After their escape from Nazi-occupied Austria to Vermont, Maria turned her eye to bees as well as children.

Morgan Freeman: Turned his Mississippi ranch into a honeybee haven to bolster the bee population rather than harvest their honey.

Winnie the Pooh: Not a keeper, but an enthusiastic consumer of honey and purveyor of bee wisdom.

ESSENTIAL INSECTS

It's impossible to exaggerate the importance of bees: they pollinate the planet's plant life, have an essential place in the ecosystem and play a pivotal role in the production of many of our foods. Later in this book, we cover the many ways we can help bees, but in this chapter we take a quick look at how bees help us. While we explore the benefits of bees, it's important to remember that it's their intrinsic worth that's most valuable of all: these beautiful creatures have carved out a niche in our world, and we must do all we can to help them flourish.

Top pollinators

Around 90 per cent of the world's wildflowers rely on pollination by animals, rather than wind or water. Although bees aren't the only creatures doing the work – butterflies, moths, wasps, beetles and even some birds and bats help out – they are nature's prime pollinators and are completely dependent on nectar and pollen for survival. Bees are unusual in that they feed pollen and nectar directly to their larvae too, so they need a good supply.

Honeybees visit up to 100 flowers every time they leave the hive and may do this 15 or more times a day, but solitary bees outperform their social cousins when it comes to pollinating. With no "pollen baskets" on their legs, they end up scattering much more pollen around. An enormous variety of bee species has evolved to support our planet's huge variety of plants, and that's why it's essential we maintain this diversity. Losing one type of plant or bee can mean the loss of the organism it has adapted to support.

BEES WORK FOR MAN; AND YET THEY NEVER BRUISE THEIR MASTER'S FLOWER.

GEORGE HERBERT

Agricultural assistance

Because of their pollinating skills, bees play an absolutely crucial role in agriculture – pollinating many of our major crops as well as fruit, vegetables and even plants used as feed for cattle. It's estimated that bees contribute over $70 billion a year to the world economy, including £500 million a year to UK agriculture, while the work of honeybees alone is worth over $15 billion to the US economy.

Seventy out of the 90 main crops grown for human consumption are dependent on bee pollination and an astonishing one-third of the food we eat – one forkful in three – has been pollinated by bees and other creatures. Some crops – blueberries and almonds, for example – rely almost entirely on bees to bear fruit.

Even plants that can self-pollinate (such as strawberries) have been shown to yield bigger fruit that stay fresher for longer if bees have had a hand (or leg!) in the process. Without bees as pollinators, supermarkets would only be able to provide half of the fruits and vegetables that are currently commonly available, and the long-term effects could be disastrous.

JUST A FEW OF THE FOODS WE'D LOSE IF BEES BECAME EXTINCT:

BLUEBERRIES	NUTS	AVOCADOS
ALMONDS	BEANS	APPLES
CHERRIES	MELONS	CUCUMBERS
HONEY	GRAPEFRUITS	BROCCOLI

In some parts of the world – Hanyuan in China for example – the bee population has seen such a decline that farmers have had to resort to painstakingly hand-pollinating crops using paint brushes and pots of pollen, while in the Netherlands small drones are being developed to take over the work of bees. These options are obviously not ideal – or economically efficient.

Ecologically essential

It's easy to see why the loss of bees would be catastrophic – we couldn't survive without pollinators – but their extinction would have an impact well beyond their role in providing the food we eat. Bees and other pollinators are part of our planet's delicately balanced ecosystem. If a bee species dies out, the plants and trees that depend on it are affected too; in turn the creatures who feed or live on those plants are affected and so on up the food chain.

Bees have an essential place in the web of life. Magpies, starlings, robins and great tits often catch them – they can remove bees' stings by rubbing them on branches before eating them. Hornets may feed on bees too, although honeybees will work together to tackle hornet intruders in the hive by forming a ball around them and killing them with the heat from their combined beating wings!

In tropical climes, a whole family of birds – the bee-eaters – depend on them for food, while in Europe, honey buzzards are so well adapted for digging into bee and wasp nests that they have special protective feathers on their face. Bears, too, love honey and will also snack on bees and their larvae.

In Africa, honey badgers forage for bees' nests to eat the honeycomb and bee larvae, and European badgers and hedgehogs do this too. Meanwhile, one African bird has a very interesting relationship with humans, bees and their nests. The honeyguide bird is able to locate wild bee nests but cannot break into them, so has learned to lead humans to the nests and wait for them to do the hard work. Once the nest is open, they feed on any wax and larvae left behind. This symbiotic relationship between human and bird has evolved over thousands of years. Bees play such a pivotal part in the finely balanced web of life that their loss would have a huge impact on our ecosystem.

Apitherapy

We benefit from bees in other ways too. Apitherapy is the name given to the use of bee products in healing, and it has gained more of a following recently as science has caught up with tradition and proved how effective these natural remedies can be.

NOTE: Do not use apitherapy products if you have an allergy to bee stings.

HONEY

Packed with enzymes, amino acids, minerals and vitamins, honey has impressive medicinal properties. Thanks to its antibacterial qualities, the ancients all used honey for treating wounds, and it remains an excellent home remedy today – in 2007, the US FDA approved manuka honey for this use. It soothes cuts and minor burns, and speeds up healing – to try this yourself, apply honey to a dressing with clean hands, and cover your wound. Honey is also an antioxidant and anti-inflammatory. It's an excellent treatment for coughs and sore throats – proven to be as effective as prescribed medicines, while being cheap, natural, easily available, and less likely to cause side effects. Take a teaspoon by itself, or add to hot water with lemon and ginger for a soothing drink.

Good for the gut, honey is a fantastic natural source of energy that doesn't leave you with a blood sugar dip afterward. A teaspoonful a day has been proven to benefit blood sugar and cholesterol levels, as well as the immune system and body weight. There are plenty of ideas for including honey in your diet in Chapter 7. It's always best to use raw honey if possible as pasteurized supermarket products will not include so many beneficial substances.

MANUKA HONEY

Manuka honey is only produced in New Zealand, where bees feed on manuka blossom, so it's more expensive than traditional types. Studies have shown it to be an even more effective healer than other types of honey thanks to a special antibacterial substance found in this honey alone.

PROPOLIS

Propolis is a sticky substance made by bees from tree sap and used to repair their hive. It has proven antibacterial qualities and can speed the healing of wounds. It's an effective treatment for bad breath and cold sores, and has anti-fungal qualities too.

ROYAL JELLY

Traditionally used in treating menopausal symptoms and anti-aging, royal jelly is a nutrient-rich form of food produced for larvae who will become queen bees. Scientific research backs up these traditional uses and there's also evidence that royal jelly improves physical and mental function in the elderly. Royal jelly is usually taken in capsule form.

BEE VENOM

The Greek physician Hippocrates used bee venom to treat joint pain and there have been promising studies that support its use in arthritis treatment today. Very recent research showed that bee venom is effective in preventing the growth of cancer cells.

BEE POLLEN

Bee pollen is believed to be anti-inflammatory, treat **PMS** symptoms and improve athletic performance; however, there have been relatively few tests into its effectiveness, and there have been signs of some rare side effects, too. It may interfere with other medicines, so – while most of us can enjoy a spoonful on our porridge or in a smoothie – do your research before trying this one out.

Beeswax

Another valuable hive product, beeswax has long been used in the production of candles, which are prized for their warm, bright flame and long burning time. Beeswax forms a natural protective barrier, which is why this versatile substance makes an appearance in everything from food production (the wax around Edam cheese) to adding a shine to polishes and beauty products. It's a natural exfoliator and leaves skin and hair feeling soft and smooth, too. (See page 121 for ideas on how to use beeswax in your own beauty treatments.)

Beneficial beekeeping

Beekeeping is an activity that benefits bees and beekeepers alike. Bees are nurtured by their keeper, who provides them with a safe home and environment, and can supplement their food during leaner months. In turn, beekeepers get the chance to reconnect with nature and the cycle of the seasons, but there are larger-scale benefits to keeping bees, too. Farmers in Africa, for example, have made use of the fact that elephants are deterred by the sound of bees, and constructed "bee fences" with hives spaced along them at 10 m (30 ft) intervals to protect their crops. A successful trial in Kenya showed that 96 per cent of the time, elephants were deterred by these fences. This scheme not only protects the farmers' assets but the elephants, too, as they would otherwise be in danger of being shot for their crop incursions.

There are also many initiatives and projects that encourage beekeeping as a way of bringing social and educational benefits to communities, while encouraging bee diversity and meeting sustainable goals at the same time. These charities change people's lives for the better by offering them the chance to learn a new skill. The schemes may provide community hives and education programmes or offer individuals the lifeline of a hive of their own and the opportunity to sell their bee products. Even better, by supporting these charities, we're also supporting bees – see beesfordevelopment.org, www.planetbee.org or www. beesabroad.org.uk for more information.

BEES UNDER
THREAT

Globally, bees and other pollinators are in serious decline: one in ten of the wild bee species in Europe is in danger of extinction; one in four of native species in America is under threat, and 35 species of bee are currently endangered in the UK, with 20 having been lost in the last century. In this chapter we discover what has caused this decline, and take a look at some positive steps we can all take to help reverse the trend.

Causes of the decline

There's no single reason for the dramatic decline in bee numbers seen in the past few decades; a number of factors have combined to make life very hard indeed for bees. Sadly, we must take the blame for causing these stressors – albeit inadvertently – but the good news is that with renewed awareness and understanding of what has gone wrong, we can move on to make informed decisions and take positive action to provide prime conditions for our pollinators.

HABITAT LOSS

The way we use our land has had a detrimental effect on bees, and one key factor is intensive farming. The loss of meadows and hedgerows to provide space for monoculture crops leaves bees struggling to find enough resources to survive. Urban development has added to the problem. With 97 per cent of wildflower meadows being lost in the UK in the past century, it's easy to see why this is an issue.

We often forget that bees can only feed on the *blossoms* of plants and trees, not roots and leaves as other insects can. They need a variety of different sources of nectar within a kilometre or so of their nest to prosper, and it's becoming increasingly hard for bees to find the nutrition they need, or a route between suitable sources.

Large-scale solutions include ensuring that new developments are sensitively placed and include bee-friendly habitats, and leaving uncropped field margins and wildlife strips on farmland: bees benefit from the foraging space and the farmer will enjoy the benefits of visiting pollinators and natural pest control. Individually, we can get together with our neighbours and plant "bee streets" – a series of neighbouring wildflower patches – in towns, or support projects that provide wildlife corridors. There are many other green spaces in our communities that can be made bee-friendly too – roadsides, parks, sports areas, school grounds and community gardens. Campaigning to leave these unmown or to cultivate wildflower banks in these places are also positive steps in the right direction.

USE OF PESTICIDES

Recent research has shown the adverse effect pesticides can have on bees, with different chemicals affecting their ability to fly and to reproduce, or making them more vulnerable to infection and disease. One particular group – the neonicotinoids – have been shown to damage bees' nervous systems and brain development, and have been banned for outside use by the EU (although in some places this is still used).

Pesticides aren't the only chemicals that bees have to contend with. Weedkillers are used on farmland too – and in many other green spaces – and all of these substances have been around for decades. Today, there's a greater awareness of the problems that pesticides cause pollinators, and plenty of advice for farmers on how to reduce their use and minimize the damage that crop-spraying causes, such as leaving unsprayed buffer zones around crops. Of course, buying organic produce, if you can, will mean that you're supporting a pollinator-friendly producer, and don't forget to make sure that the products you use in your garden are chemical free. (Some bulbs are sprayed with neonicotinoids, for example, which could damage the bees on your patch.) See page 94 for information on how to make your own garden bee friendly.

CLIMATE CHANGE

Warming temperatures and shifting seasons have created further problems for bees, as plants blossom at different times. Bees can end up emerging before the blossom they depend upon is available, or too late to find it, and this can also have a knock-on effect for plants that need pollination, such as fruit trees. Meanwhile, our warming climate means that many species across the planet are being forced to move northward in order to adjust, but scientists believe that bees find it difficult to adapt in this way.

PESTS AND DISEASES

Pests and diseases are a major cause of concern in honeybee colonies in particular, as they can spread so quickly in the close confines of the hive. Varroa mites, for example, are a big problem for commercial beekeepers and have been identified as one of the major causes of Colony Collapse Disorder, the name given to the drastic increase in failed beehives noticed in the past 20 years. Nowadays beekeepers can expect to lose 50 per cent of their hives, as opposed to 5–10 per cent back in the 1990s. Diseases spread by pests can also affect bumblebees and other wild bees, so good beekeeping practice is important in safeguarding them, too. There's plenty of online advice for keeping hives disease free – including frequently cleaning hive equipment and regularly inspecting and replacing combs.

INVASIVE SPECIES

The arrival of an invasive non-native species, such as the Asian hornet – a fierce predator of bees – could decimate bee colonies in the UK and US. Scientists in the US are using thermal imaging cameras to search for nests. It's important to report any sightings of these insects. In the UK, contact the NNSS, which provides plenty of information on identification, at www.nonnativespecies. org. In the US, visit www.invasivespeciesinfo.gov for more information.

POLLUTION

Air pollution – traffic fumes in particular – can mask or change the smell of flowers, making it harder for bees to find them. In fact, anything that hinders bees from navigating or foraging properly can have a really detrimental effect. Light pollution is also an issue: street lighting deters night-time pollinators from doing their work, so fewer blossoms are available during the day for bees to feed on, and light at night-time also disrupts their natural cycles, which can affect reproduction.

Taking action

While it may seem that we can't do much as individuals to tackle some of these bigger issues, we can certainly work together with others to raise awareness about them and bring about change. If you're passionate about bees, spread the love. Share your knowledge – fascinating facts and a few scary stats – and see if you can encourage your friends and family to become bee-friendly too. You could engage in a little positive bee PR: explain that most bees don't sting, for example, or that honeybees in a swarm are simply looking for a new place to nest, they're not out to attack.

Friends of the Earth, Greenpeace and other charities are working hard to raise awareness of the problems bees are facing. Supporting these groups is one way of helping bees – through fundraising, membership and signing petitions, or simply following them on social media and sharing campaign details. (Searching for the hashtag "#savethebees" will lead you to all the latest posts.)

Read all you can about bees in your area to see what factors are affecting them locally, and look out for action groups to see if a plan is in place to help. Search for "bee corridor" initiatives and see if you can help with establishing these, or consider supporting beekeeping projects (see page 74), which give something back to the community as well as bees.

There are also bee projects that businesses can support – by either adopting a hive or sponsoring one – to improve their green credentials. Bees for Business in the UK and Planet Bee Foundation in the US have more information on this. If you have children or contacts with local schools, beekeeping can be a wonderful extra-curricular activity, suitable for all ages with the correct supervision.

You may not be able to go as far as gifting a hive to a friend, but buying honey from local organic producers is a great way of supporting good beekeeping. In fact, there are plenty of consumer choices you can make that benefit bees: buying food supplies from local producers means that you're supporting smaller, less intensively farmed initiatives, which are far better for our pollinators. Some producers who promote pollinator well-being label their items as bee- or pollinator-friendly too, so look out for these. You can even keep bees in mind when purchasing cotton items: cotton is a crop that's notorious for the use of pesticides in its production, so organic cotton is much better where bees are concerned.

A rewarding way of helping bees in your area is by joining a bee walk with fellow enthusiasts or carrying out a bit of solo citizen science: take a regular stroll during the spring or summer and look out for bees, recording those you see. Friends of the Earth, the Bumblebee Conservation Trust, www.aussiebee.com.au and bumblebee.org all have handy bee identification guides on hand to help, and – in the UK – you can upload your data to the Bumblebee Conservation Trust to help form a picture of bee numbers in your patch.

A GOOD BEE NEVER LANDS ON A FALLEN FLOWER.

CHINESE PROVERB

A little hope

Bees have faced mass extinction before and come back from the brink. There's DNA evidence that 65 million years ago – when the dinosaurs went extinct and flowering plants were in serious decline – bees were also hit by a dip in numbers, and countless other insect species died out. As larger mammals evolved to fill the niche left by the dinosaurs, some larger species of bees – including early bumblebees – evolved and flourished. This gives us hope that it may be possible to restore the current balance and avert an ecological crisis.

Although the threat is serious, the good news is that there's a lot we can do to help bees and other pollinators, and we're already making some steps in the right direction. The widespread realization that we're facing a crisis has led to some pro-bee policy making. DEFRA has announced their bee plan for 2030 in the UK, which includes a commitment to restoring wildlife-rich habitat and giving beekeepers access to free advice and resources to help them practise good bee husbandry. The European

Environment Agency and US Environmental Protection Agency have banned the use of some damaging pesticides, and a general move toward ecological farming in Europe – farming organically and banning the use of genetically modified crops – will help protect pollinators and support the biodiversity that is essential for bees to prosper.

Recent reports from experts in the UK, Europe and the US show that the loss of biodiversity has slowed, and that the fate of some solitary bees and plants has even improved as the eco-awareness of the past couple of decades starts to have an effect. But there's a long way to go. We need to take decisive action at every level to nurture and protect bees and other pollinators – from the choices we make as individuals to decisions on international policy. Turn to Chapter 6 for practical suggestions on how you can make a real difference to these brilliant and beautiful creatures.

HOW TO LOOK AFTER BEES

There's so much you can do to look after your local bees – and you don't need green fingers to do it. Bees need a few basics to survive – a safe place to nest, a variety of pollens and nectar to feed on, and (for bumblebee queens) somewhere to spend the winter – and you can help them to find all of these things more easily. This chapter includes plenty of practical ideas for looking after our favourite pollinators, as well as a basic introduction to keeping honeybees, in case you're looking to make 50,000 new friends!

Plant flowers... or herbs... or hedges...

The most important thing we can do to support bees is to provide them with a supply of pollen and nectar: planting a variety of flowers in your garden, yard or window box is a great way to do this. Wildflower mixes are effective as they include a selection of plants that bees love: just like us, bees need a varied diet. It's easy to get hold of a pack – from a garden centre or bee-friendly charity – which you can simply sprinkle, water and enjoy. Bees prefer native blooms, but exotic plants can provide nectar when their favourites are thin on the ground.

There's plenty of information online about choosing bee-friendly plants to suit your outdoor space, whether it's shady, dry or sunny – and many plants are labelled "bee friendly" in garden centres – but here are a few pointers:

- Bees are particularly attracted to purple flowers, so groups of buddleia, lavender and alliums are good options.

- Bulbs are another good choice as they're hardy – plant them in the autumn to feed your bees in spring.
- Go for single blooms rather than double ones, so that bees can access the nectar easily.
- Tubular flowers – such as snapdragons and foxgloves – are a favourite of bumblebees.

Some bees need to find pollen and nectar all year round, even in the colder months, so try to make sure you have plants in flower throughout the year. Heather has a long flowering season, while hellebores, snowdrops and winter-flowering honeysuckle will provide pollen in the winter. Rosemary is good too, as bees love it and it flowers for most of the year – in fact many herbs appeal to bees, as they're so fragrant. Remember, too, that fruit and veg (such as strawberries and runner beans) have blossoms that provide food for bees: the plants benefit from pollination and will give you a crop too. If you have space for a tree, a fruit tree is an option that will benefit both you and your bees, but most trees bear blossom and can be another vital source of food.

The bee-friendly garden

If you're a reluctant gardener but keen to support pollinators, there's good news: the less manicured your garden, the better it is for bees. In fact – apart from providing pollen-rich plants – some of the best ways to make your bees feel at home in your backyard or outdoor space involve *not* doing things. Here are a few ideas:

- Leave piles of leaves or patches of bare soil to give solitary bees somewhere to nest.
- Allow a few weeds that will provide native blossoms for visiting bees.
- Mow your lawn less often and avoid weedkiller and artificial fertilizers, allowing bee-friendly clover and dandelions to grow.
- Leave a patch of lawn completely unmown all year round, giving ground-nesting bumblebees a place to nest.
- Make your compost heap a safe place for nesting bees by leaving it undisturbed.

- Don't water your garden until evening, so that bees don't get waterlogged when foraging for nectar during the day. Water at the base of plants if you can.

If you're feeling more industrious, you could pile up a few logs to create another nesting habitat or make a bee hotel or two (see page 98). Bees may use bird nesting boxes if you have them, while adding a pond to your garden will benefit insects, birds and small mammals. This will provide a water source for them, and bees can nest in the damp sand or soil around its edges. You can also plant bee-friendly flowers around your pond, such as water mint or irises.

If you don't have a garden or outdoor space, planting up a window box with a couple of bee-friendly plants is a valuable alternative, or how about planning a community project – a simple wildflower patch on an unused piece of ground or shared space could provide pollen for bees and boost the well-being of everyone involved, too.

Provide a water source

Water is important for bees – in hot weather, honeybees carry water back to the hive where their fellow workers distribute it and it cools the hive through evaporation. This water-powered air-con helps maintain the hive's optimum temperature. And solitary bees need water too, drinking from muddy puddles or damp, slimy stones to get additional hydration.

Getting water can be problematic for bees – they need a really shallow source to drink from safely, or they risk getting waterlogged. Bird baths can be too deep, and gathering water from natural sources, such as rivers and ponds, can be even more risky, so give your bee visitors a safe place to rehydrate and you'll be doing them a great service.

One easy option is to fill a flan tin or saucer with marbles or pebbles, add water and then leave in your garden or on a windowsill. The marbles give bees a safe place to land without any risk of drowning. Alternatively, use a deeper dish and float small pieces of wood or wine corks on the water for your bees to land on. As bees navigate by smell, you may want to add a very small amount of white sugar to your water until the bees have discovered it. Once they've found your watering hole, though, tap water will be fine, as the bees will remember its location – and honeybees will tell their sisters about it too!

Building bee hotels

You may have seen bee hotels for sale, but making one yourself is a simple and satisfying project. The classic design includes a selection of hollow bamboo canes, grasses or reeds, and will appeal to solitary bees. Try to include a range of different-width holes. Trim your materials to the same length, smooth off any uneven ends with sandpaper and seal one end of each tube with modelling clay. Then cut the ends off a plastic bottle to form a cylinder and pack your canes inside. Use garden twine to hang it somewhere safe, out of the wind, and keep an eye on your bee hotel – sealed-up canes mean that bees have moved in!

You can build different types of hotel to suit different species of bee. Bumblebees will often look for disused rodent nests as they like to overwinter underground, but you can build them an alternative. Choose a dry, shaded area and place a 30 x 30 cm (12 x 12 in.) square of chicken wire on the ground, raised up on some stones. Top this with some pet bedding material for the nesting area. Pierce a length of hosepipe – measuring at least 30 cm (12 in.) long and 18 mm (¾ in.) in diameter – at regular intervals and then place this along the ground, holes facing downward, embedded a little and leading into the nesting area. Cover the nesting area with an upturned terracotta pot (at least 20 cm/8 in. in diameter), making sure that one end of the hose leads into the pot – this is the bees' entrance tunnel. Cover the length of pipe with soil, leaving just the end exposed at ground level. Place a piece of slate on top of the upturned pot, raised up on stones, to act as a rain cover.

Once finished, leave your bumblebee nest undisturbed – and don't despair if a mouse sets up home inside first... Bumblebee queens will be attracted to the scent and use the nest site in following years. Other items can be substituted, and you can improvise with various materials such as bricks, sticks, cones and recycled pallets, as long as you provide a covered nesting area and access.

Looking out for bees

BEE FIRST AID

It's useful to know what to do if you find a "grounded" bumblebee. Often these bees, usually queens, are simply resting and won't need help – but if a bee has been on the ground for 40 minutes or more, they may be in trouble and need help to get airborne again. Gently move your bee (using a leaf or credit card) to a nearby bee-friendly flower to feed. If there are no blooms available, you could mix up some sugar water – 50:50 white sugar to water – as a last-resort energy boost. Offer the sugar water on the tip of a teaspoon, and be careful not to get your bee's fur or wings sticky. (Never feed a bee honey, which can contain pathogens, or brown sugar, which they can't easily digest.) Sadly, if your bee has a disease or is at the end of her life – look for ragged wings – there will be little you can do to revive her.

SEEING A SWARM

A swarm of honeybees may appear intimidating, but the bees aren't out to attack – a swarm happens when a hive gets overcrowded and the queen and half of her workers decide it's time to start again elsewhere, leaving behind a new queen with the rest of the colony. Bees in a swarm will have fed well before leaving to look for pastures new and aren't defending a hive or honey stores, so they will be much more docile than usual. If you see a swarm, don't panic: contact the British Beekeepers Association (in the UK) or the American Beekeeping Federation (in the US) for advice – their volunteers can remove honeybee swarms safely. Think of it as a great privilege if you're lucky enough to see a swarm of these miraculous insects.

FINDING A NEST

If you find a bumblebee nest on your property, the best thing to do is leave it in peace. Bumblebees aren't aggressive and will just want to go about their bee business undisturbed. The only time they can become defensive is if they feel their nest is under threat, so don't get too close – you may want to put up a barrier to stop children or pets taking an interest. Try to see your bee visitors as a blessing and remember that bee colonies only last for a few months, so they won't be a long-term nuisance. The Bumblebee Conservation Organisation advises against moving nests: it may be possible to provide bees with a different entrance rather than trying to relocate – or worse, destroy – the nest.

Beekeeping basics

TO BEEKEEP, OR NOT TO BEEKEEP

Beekeeping offers you the chance to build a unique relationship with a colony of wild creatures. It's absorbing and relaxing, will help you to reconnect with the natural world, is a way of supporting pollinators and the environment... and you'll have your own supply of delicious honey, should you want to harvest it. An established hive can produce 18-27 kg (40-60 lb) of honey per year, but before you order your bee suit, there are a few things to consider.

Keeping bees takes time and commitment: you'll spend an average of 30 minutes a week on your hive – with more frequent visits in spring and summer. Beehives need to be thoroughly checked every two to three weeks, to make sure all is as it should be, so you'll need to learn to spot problems in your colony. You'll also want to learn how to prevent your bees from swarming too often. In addition to this, you're likely to do a lot of heavy lifting (depending on the type of hive you use) – and you'll definitely get a sting or two!

Think through the practicalities of your new project before you get started. Do you have somewhere flat and accessible to site your hive? It should have at least 3 m (10 ft) of undisturbed space around it and should definitely be sheltered from the wind. Where will you keep your equipment? This will be bulky, as you'll pick up spare frames and extra pieces as you progress.

There's a lot to learn, but there's also plenty of support and information out there, including dozens of books and online forums. A wonderful way to find out about beekeeping is to go on an introductory course: you'll learn about the costs, work and equipment involved, and find out how to get set up if you decide to take the plunge. Look up your local beekeeping association for more information. It's a good move to find a mentor if you can – a local beekeeper who can give you the benefit of their experience when queries come up and will know the intricacies of beekeeping in your local environment and weather conditions.

BASIC EQUIPMENT

Hives: Many beekeepers use a Langstroth hive: boxes of frames where your bees will live and store their honey. These hives often produce strong yields, but lifting full boxes can be heavy work. An alternative is the top-bar hive, where you'll only need to lift out single bars of comb. The Modified National is the most popular hive in the UK, and comes with the option of a mesh floor, which aids ventilation. Whichever hive you use, it should have a sturdy stand.

Bees: You can either buy your first "nucleus" of bees from an established beekeeper or order them online. (These will be ready in spring, but you will need to pre-order during the winter.) Spring is a good time to start beekeeping, as you get to know your colony during the summer as it grows, and may even be able to harvest some honey by August.

> Equipment can be costly to buy new, so it's a good idea to pick up quality second-hand equipment when you're starting out, while you make sure beekeeping is for you.

Protective clothing: A bee suit is essential, as is a veil. (Suits are always white as bees react aggressively toward anyone wearing dark clothing.) An all-in-one suit is best as this won't leave any gaps for bees to seek out. You'll need gloves and gauntlets too – go for the best quality you can afford – and it's a good idea to wear boots, so that you can tuck your suit safely into them. ALWAYS wear your veil when tending to your bees.

Hive tool: You'll use this handy tool every time you inspect your hive, to prize out frames that have become glued up with propolis, or to remove unwanted comb. A tool with a J-shaped end is useful.

Bee smoker: Another essential, a bee smoker will pacify your bees and allow you to work on the hive without them mounting an attack. The smoke stops the bees smelling the alarm pheromone released by guard bees when someone approaches the hive.

There's more equipment to discover as you establish your colony, but these basics will get you up and running.

ONE CAN NO MORE APPROACH
PEOPLE WITHOUT LOVE
THAN ONE CAN APPROACH
BEES WITHOUT CARE. SUCH
IS THE QUALITY OF BEES.

LEO TOLSTOY

THE BEEKEEPER'S YEAR

Winter: A quiet time as bees wait for spring. In cold climes, you may need to wrap your hives to keep them warm. Read beekeeping books and pre-order new bees if necessary.

Spring: As flowers burst into bloom your bees become active. Start regular inspections of your hive and get ready to control swarms. Harvest excess honey left over from winter… or feed your bees if they are low on supplies.

Summer: Your bees are at their busiest, so check them regularly. Harvest excess honey, which will be darker and stronger in flavour than in spring.

Autumn: The prime time for your honey harvest – be sure to leave enough for your bees to overwinter. Plan ahead for the colder months by providing extra food if necessary.

SAFETY

Bear in mind that your colony can have off days, so always wear your protective clothing, and remember that even black socks can rile your bees! Keep an antihistamine cream on hand, and act quickly if you do get stung – swiftly remove the bee's sting with a credit card or similar.

HONEY RECIPES AND BEESWAX CRAFTS

Honey and beeswax are versatile hive products and this chapter includes ideas on how to use them in cooking, craft and beauty projects. From speedy pick-me-ups and simple recipes to more elaborate bakes, there are plenty of tasty ways to benefit from honey's natural nutrients. It's a beneficial ingredient in beauty products too, so read on to discover how to make your own soap, facial scrub and lip balm. And if you're feeling crafty, you can try your hand at making beeswax candles and food wraps, too. Be sure to buy your wax and honey from a sustainable source.

Buying honey

When buying honey, opt for raw local products if possible: they will retain more nutritional benefits than pasteurized honey. It's surprising how honeys made from different nectar can have quite distinctive tastes – generally, darker products have a richer flavour. (Note: honey should not be given to children less than a year old, as it can cause toxins to build up in their gut.)

If you're buying honey from a store, take care: some shop-bought products in the US contain additives such as corn syrup, and lack the nutritional benefits of the genuine product. In the EU, products with these additives cannot be labelled "honey".

If your honey crystallizes, this is perfectly normal. You can use it as it is, or to return it to a smoother state, just stand the jar in a bowl of warm water. (Don't microwave it or it will lose a lot of its nutritional goodness.)

> Honey burns at higher temperatures, so cook honey-based dishes at a low or medium heat if you can.

BEES HAVE SO
MUCH TO OFFER US,
IF WE ONLY LISTEN.

JAY EBBEN

Quick honey fixes

HONEY AND CINNAMON TEA

This tasty tea combines the immune-boosting, infection-busting benefits of two superfoods. It can help with the treatment of mild bladder infections and benefits the complexion, too. Simply stir 3–4 teaspoons of raw honey into a mug of boiled water that you've left to cool for a moment. Add 1 teaspoon of ground cinnamon, stir and enjoy.

HOT TODDY

If you want to give your usual cold remedy a kick, add a couple of tablespoons of whisky into your hot-water-and-honey mix. Stir in a slice of lemon, and add your favourite spice to taste, such as ginger, cinnamon, cloves or nutmeg.

HONEY HANGOVER CURE

The fructose in honey helps to neutralize the negative impact of alcohol on the body. A *really* quick fix is to eat toast with honey and sliced bananas. Alternatively, make a smoothie using honey, bananas, milk and a dash of cream.

HONEY DRESSING (SERVES 2)

Honey and balsamic vinegar make a great pairing, so whisk up a tasty salad dressing with 1 tablespoon each of honey and olive oil, 2 tablespoons of balsamic vinegar and 1 teaspoon of wholegrain mustard. Season to taste.

HONEY SOY MARINADE (SERVES 3–4)

Whisk together 1 large garlic clove (crushed), and 3 tablespoons each of sesame oil, soy sauce, lemon juice and honey to make a great marinade for your choice of meat or fish. If you have time, marinate overnight, but if not, it will still taste delicious added just before cooking.

HONEY FUDGE SAUCE (SERVES 4)

A great complement to ice cream, this sauce is easy to make by melting the ingredients – 75 g (2½ oz) brown sugar, 25 g (1 oz) butter, 2 tablespoons honey and 60 ml (2 fl oz) evaporated milk – in a bowl over a pan of boiling water. Cool and store in the fridge for up to a month. Warm to serve. For a chocolatey sauce, substitute 40 g (1½ oz) chocolate chips for the sugar.

Easy honey cake
(makes 12 generous servings)

This recipe for honey cake is tasty, easy to make and saves on washing-up, as it's prepared using just one pan.

INGREDIENTS:

150 g (5 oz) butter
100 g (3½ oz) soft brown sugar
150 ml (5 fl oz) honey
1 tablespoon milk
2 eggs
200 g (7 oz) self-raising flour
Flaked almonds and 2 tablespoons honey to
    garnish, optional

Preheat the oven to 180°C (350°F) and line a rectangular cake tin, approximately 28 x 18 x 5 cm (11 x 7 x 2 in.). Melt together the butter, sugar and honey over a low heat, stirring in the milk to make a smooth mix. Remove pan from heat and allow to cool. Gradually beat in the eggs and then fold in the flour. Sprinkle over the almonds, if using, and bake for 30 minutes or until the cake has risen. Turn out, brush with 2 tablespoons of warmed honey to glaze, and leave to cool. This cake will keep for up to five days in an airtight tin... if you haven't eaten it by then!

Honey makes a great substitute for sugar in most recipes. Not only does it have a lower GI value than sugar, but it means moister bakes, too. Honey is sweeter than sugar, so you won't need to use as much of it – and you'll need to slightly reduce the amount of liquid in your recipe to account for it being moister.

NOTE: Honey will slide off the spoon if you dip the spoon in hot water first.

Honey biscuits
(makes 24 biscuits)

A great accompaniment to cheese, or spread with butter, these biscuits are simple to make but taste wonderful. Wholewheat flour makes them a healthier option.

INGREDIENTS:

225 g (8 oz) wholewheat flour
½ teaspoon salt
100 g (3½ oz) butter at room temperature
2 tablespoons honey

Mix the flour and salt in a bowl, then rub in the butter between your fingertips. Stir in the honey, then roll out the mixture on a floured surface. Cut into rounds with a biscuit cutter or upturned glass. Bake at 150°C (300°F) for 20 minutes or until golden brown.

Honey energy balls
(makes 18 balls)

A brilliant way of getting your daily honey hit, these energy balls are a nutritional powerhouse as they also include fibre (from the oats), healthy fats (from the nut butter) and superfood add-ins (such as dried fruit or dark chocolate).

INGREDIENTS:

125 g (4½ oz) rolled oats
2 tablespoons seeds, such as chia or flax
120 g (4¼ oz) peanut butter
115 g (4 oz) honey
80 g (2¾ oz) dark chocolate chips
1 teaspoon vanilla extract
Salt

Mix together all the ingredients in a bowl to form a sticky dough, seasoning to taste. (Add more peanut butter if your mixture is too dry, or more oats if it's too wet.) Chill in the fridge for 30 minutes, then roll into 2.5 cm (1 in.) balls. Keep in the fridge for up to 2 weeks.

Honey beauty tips

Honey's special properties make it a valuable addition to skincare products: it's antibacterial and good for cleansing; it restores and retains moisture levels in the skin, leaving it wonderfully soft; and it soothes inflammation. Here are some easy ways to bring a touch of honey magic to your beauty routine.

To remove make-up mix 1 teaspoon of pure honey into 3 tablespoons of coconut oil to create a gentle cleanser that's perfect for sensitive skin. Store at room temperature.

Mix together 2 teaspoons each of honey and ground almonds to make a facial scrub that exfoliates and leaves your skin feeling moisturized too.

Enjoy a soothing bath soak by mixing 30 g (1 oz) honey with 500 ml (1 pint) milk. Add a few drops of lavender essential oil and pour into a hot bath.

Stir a tablespoon of honey into a litre (2 pints) of warm water and rinse through hair after washing. Leave this conditioner on for half an hour before rinsing for super soft and shiny results.

HONEY LIP BALM

This soothing lip balm combines the protective power of beeswax with the healing properties of honey. Melt 3 teaspoons of organic beeswax pellets with 5 teaspoons of jojoba oil in a glass bowl over a pan of simmering water. Remove from the heat and stir in 1 teaspoon of honey and a couple of drops of peppermint essential oil (if you like). Mix thoroughly so that the honey is blended in well. Pour into small containers and leave to cool.

HONEY SOAP

You can add honey to any soap recipe and you can even buy soap moulds in the shape of honeycombs. A nice easy method is to use a melt-and-pour goat's milk soap base. Cut half a block of the soap base (500 g/1 lb) into squares and melt in a double boiler. Stir in 2–3 tablespoons of honey and add a few drops of vitamin E oil. Pour into moulds and leave to cool. These gentle soaps make a fragrant and creamy lather, and are perfect gifts.

Beeswax candles
(makes 3 medium-sized candles)

These environmentally friendly candles burn for longer than paraffin-based candles, clean your air (by releasing negative ions) and will fill a corner of your home with a warm glow and the gentle scent of honey.

YOU WILL NEED:

3 sturdy candle wicks
Glue dots or double-sided tape
3 x 200 ml mason jars
500 g (1 lb) beeswax pellets
120 ml (4 fl oz) coconut oil
A pencil and sticky tape

1. Firmly attach the wicks to the base of your jars. Beeswax is slow burning, so you will need thick, sturdy wicks for this project.

2. Melt the wax and oil in a double boiler or in a glass bowl over a pan of simmering water. Stir until the wax is thoroughly melted and combined.

3. Pour the wax into the jars around the wick, then make sure that the wick is centred while the wax cools. To do this, balance a pencil across the top of the jar and secure the wick to it with sticky tape.

4. Allow the candles to cool in a warm place – the wax may crack if they're cooled too quickly. If a dip appears when the wax contracts, melt a little more wax and top up. Trim the wick to about 7 mm (¼ in.).

You can, of course, use different sized jars or containers to make your candles. This project would make two 280 ml jar candles, or six 100 ml candles, for example.

How to make beeswax wraps

These food wraps make the most of the anti-bacterial properties of beeswax and are an eco-friendly alternative to cling film. They can be refreshed and reused any number of times.

YOU WILL NEED:

100 per cent cotton fabric

An iron

Pinking shears

Ruler, pencil and tape measure

Baking parchment

Beeswax pellets (pure or cosmetic-grade)

1. Wash and iron your fabric to remove any shiny coating that could prevent the wax from being absorbed. Beeswax can add a yellow tinge to material, so bear this in mind when choosing your fabric.

2. Using pinking shears, cut your cloth into 30 x 30 cm (12 x 12 in.) squares to wrap sandwiches, or 20 x 20 cm (8 x 8 in.) squares for wrapping snacks.

3. Place your fabric square on top of a piece of baking parchment on a heatproof surface. Sprinkle with beeswax pellets and place another piece of parchment on top.

4. With your iron on a low setting, carefully melt the beeswax into the fabric. Push out the melted wax to cover the cloth evenly – don't worry if it goes over the edges.

5. Peel back the top layer of parchment paper and check that the cotton is covered. Fill in any missed areas by sprinkling on a few more pellets and ironing this in. Use the edge of the iron to push away any excess wax at the sides, then peel off the paper and allow your wrap to cool.

6. Your wraps are ready to use! Simply use the heat of your hands to mould them around whatever you want to cover. You can wash them in cool soapy water and leave to dry. If your wraps go crunchy after a while, give them a quick iron through parchment paper to restore the wax.

NOTE: The wraps aren't suitable for keeping meat fresh – they're best used to wrap sandwiches or to cover food that you'll be using in the next day.

Conclusion

I hope that this book has deepened your love and admiration for our planet's top pollinators and shown you that building a connection with them is wonderfully rewarding – for humans and bees alike. Whether you seek out local honey producers, share bee facts with your friends, create a pollinator-friendly place for them in your backyard or embark on the adventure of beekeeping, you'll be continuing a relationship that goes back thousands of years, and helping to support the amazing creatures who have made our world such a beautiful and bountiful place to live.

WHEN THE FLOWER BLOSSOMS, THE BEE WILL COME.

SRIKUMAR RAO

If you're interested in finding out more
about our books, find us on Facebook at
Summersdale Publishers, on Twitter at
@Summersdale and on Instagram at
@summersdalebooks.

www.summersdale.com

IMAGE CREDITS